Woodlands.explo

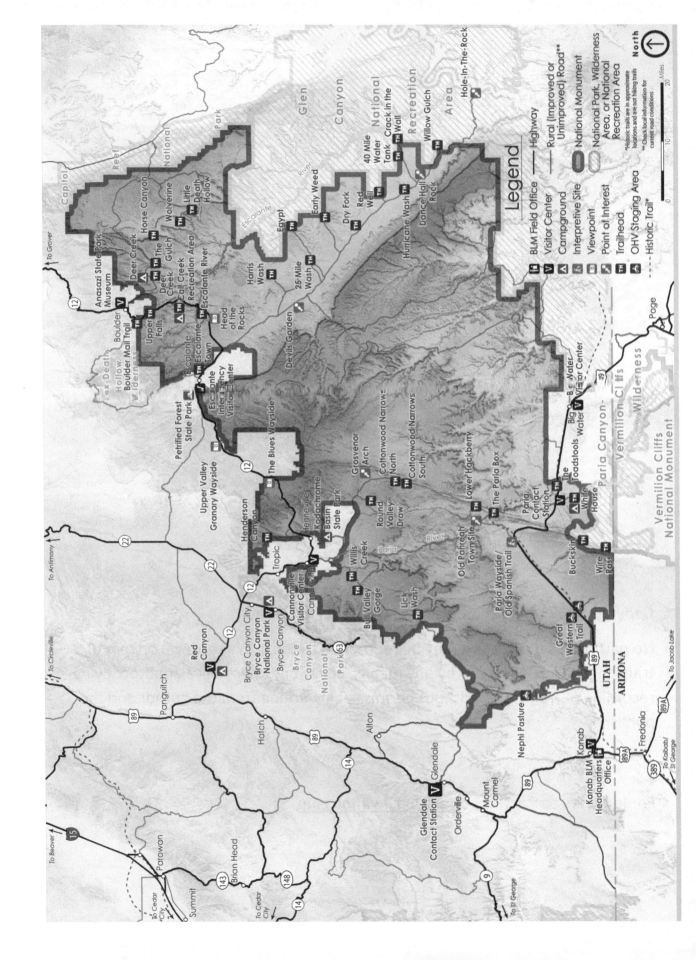

HIKING TRAILS

Lower Calf Creek Falls

The lower falls of Calf Creek were for many years one of the hidden, little visited attractions of south Utah but since the creation of Grand Staircase-Escalante National Monument they have become quite well known. At the falls, the creek emerges from a V-shaped channel at the end of upper Calf Creek Canyon and cascades over a near-vertical cliff face into a large pool several feet deep, enclosed on three sides by sheer Navajo sandstone walls. Rocks closest to the water are covered in delicate patches of blue and green algae, all the nearby cliffs have long streaks of desert varnish and the whole scene is extremely beautiful.

Although the falls are just 300 meters from UT 12, they can be viewed at this point only by a rather difficult climb down a steep gradient into the upper canyon. The usual access is along a 2.75-mile path that starts from the popular campsite at the BLM-managed Calf Creek Recreation Area - the first place where the canyon walls become less steep allowing the main road to descend to creek level, where it remains for the next one mile south until Calf Creek meets the Escalante River. In summer, the campground and parking area may fill up by early afternoon, necessitating a drive along the main road to the nearest lay-by, and consequently a longer hike.

There is little overall elevation change along the path but it has some short, steep sections, is often unshaded and has a surface of mostly soft sand so the journey can be quite strenuous, and quite a few who set out turn back before reaching the waterfall. The round trip takes 3-4 hours according to the trailguide (a useful, illustrated pamphlet describing 24 points of interest), but under 2 hours if walking quickly. The route is along the west side of the creek, generally above the canyon floor which is covered by large areas of reeds and thick grass. It passes three Indian petroglyph sites and two ruined stone-built granaries, tucked away in alcoves in cliffs at the far side. After rounding the end of a side canyon at mile 1.8, the path descends closer to the stream and is more shaded, as the canyon walls become steeper and the route passes through woodland. One section of the cliffs has especially pretty streaks of desert varnish - the colorful patination formed by gradual deposition of iron-containing minerals by evaporating rainfall.

Calf Creek Falls are heard some distance away but are hidden from view until right near the end. Either side of the main cascade, an elongated seep between two rock layers sustains a band of greenery, and there are other small pools nearby plus a large marshy area; these moist, sheltered conditions support a variety of fish and other wildlife, including beaver and quite numerous grass snakes. The falls face southeast and are quite enclosed so are in shadow for most of the day - the best time to arrive is mid-morning.

Waypoints

1

Welcome to Calf Creek!

Welcome to Calf Creek! The year-round flow of the creek begins several miles up canyon with large seeps and springs. Water is the key to survival here and this lush riparian habitat supports an abundance of plant and animal life. People have also depended on the life-giving waters of Calf Creek for thousands of years.

37.7960333, -111.4136667

2

How the canyon was formed

Water forms canyons. Over millions of years, the creek has carved its way deeper and deeper into its channel. Meanwhile, rain water flowing over cliffs and down slopes along the sides of the canyon erodes sand grains, pebbles, rocks, and boulders, gradually widening the canyon. Major erosion and sediment transport occurs when flash floods from summer thunderstorms roar down the canyon. Water and wind erosion also forms arches, alcoves, intricate honeycombing, and water pockets. Look around you and observe the wonders of water and wind at work.

37.7970345, -111.413126

3

Ponds and marshy areas

Sometimes there are ponds and marshy areas along the creek formed by beaver dams. Beavers and industrious, sometimes building large and extensive dams. Beaver dams help control flooding, reduce siltation downstream, and provide habitat for mature fish. Insects, frogs, and birds are attracted to these wetland areas, and a variety of ducks can be observed here.

37.8013667, -111.4107

4

Gambel oak

Gambel oak is an upland species. In high desert areas it is often found in cool, shady locations. The twigs, leaves, and acorns provide important food for wildlife, especially deer and turkeys.

37.8018833, -111.4110167

Watermelon farm

You wouldn't know it looking at Calf Creek today, but in the early 1900s a local farmer grew watermelons here along the banks of the creek. They were said to be "the best melons in Boulder." Floods and native vegetation, however, have removed all signs of this agricultural venture.

37.8039833, -111.41195

6

Granary

High on the cliff across the creek is a storage structure (granary) built more than 800 years ago by prehistoric people who lived in the canyons. We call this culture the Fremont. Assorted food items and seeds were stored in these structures. What would it have been like to be a Fremont Indian living in this canyon?

37.8074, -111.4113

7

Desert varnish

Millions of years ago a huge Sahara-like desert covered this area. Sand dunes hundreds of feet high drifted back and forth. The wind-blown sand of this former desert is now Navajo Sandstone. It is the predominant geologic layer found in Calf Creek Canyon and is a cliff-forming layer usually white in color. The dark streaks on the canyon walls are called desert varnish. It forms when windblown dust or rain leave behind trace amounts of iron and manganese. Rainwater combines with these minerals to create oxides, leaving behind the reddish-brown to black patina on the cliff walls. Bacteria growing on the cliff faces also contribute by concentrating these minerals and cementing the oxides to the rock surface. Over time, as desert varnish ages, it becomes thicker and darker.

37.8099833, -111.4123

8

Old fence

The old fence line is a reminder of the historic use of Calf Creek Canyon by early pioneers. Weaned calves were kept in the natural pasture created by the box canyon above the fence, hence the name "Calf Creek."

37.8116667, -111.4129167

Pictographs

Across the canyon, near the bottom of the smooth cliff wall, are three large figures painted with red pigment - further evidence that people have used Calf Creek for hundreds of years. (Pictographs are painted images while petroglyphs are carved or pecked into the rock surface.) With their trapezoidal shape, depictions of arms and legs, and elaborate head dresses, these images are typical of Fremont style rock art. Their meaning is unknown. Archaeologists speculate that it may represent significant events, religions ceremonies, deities, lineages, information, maps, or even warnings. Rock art, like all archaeological sites, are a limited resource. Once they are damaged or destroyed, they are gone forever. Please help protect and preserve this link to the past. Look, but never touch or damage rock art or prehistoric structures. These activities result in the loss of valuable scientific information and cultural connections.

37.8124833, -111.4137

10

Another storage granary

Straight ahead on the right-hand wall of this side canyon is another storage granary. The Fremont people grew corn, beans, and squash along creeks and river bottoms, but more often they relied on gathering native plants, pinyon nuts, berries, and seeds. They also fished and hunted deer, bighorn sheep, and other small mammals.

37.8133333, -111.4163

11

Horsetail and Boxelder

Horsetail is a jointed plant found only in wet areas. Pioneers called is scouring rush and used to scrub pots and pans. Boxelder, and member of the maple family, is the predominant tree in the canyon. Reaching a height of 50 feet, it grows rapidly in wet places. It provides bank stabilization for the creek and amble shade for both people and wildlife.

37.8174667, -111.4152833

12

The creek

The creek is the life force within the canyon. It provides life-sustaining water for the plants and animals here. Aquatic plants, insects, and fish make their home within the creek itself. Brook brown and rainbow trout can often be seen resting on the creek bottom or darting in and out of hiding spots under vegetation along the creek bank.

37.8246669, -111.4185548

13

Wetland ecosystems

Wetlands are one of the most productive and important ecosystems, displaying a greater abundance of plant and animal life than adjoining upland areas. A healthy riparian zone filters and purifies the water passing through it, reduces sediment loads, enhances soil stability, and contributes to ground water recharge and flow. Cattail, common reed, river birch, cottonwood, false Solomon's seal, and willow are all water-loving plants you may see in the canyon.

37.8268167, -111.4182

14

The falls

Mist from the falls and shade from the canyon walls keep the temperature cooler here. Look for scarlet monkey flower, Easter flower, and maiden hair fern growing near seeps in the cliff walls. Close your eyes and listen to the sounds of water and wind. Feel the mist on your face. Imagine how different this canyon and your hike would be without the creek. Water is precious in the desert. Water is life.

37.8286833, -111.4195833

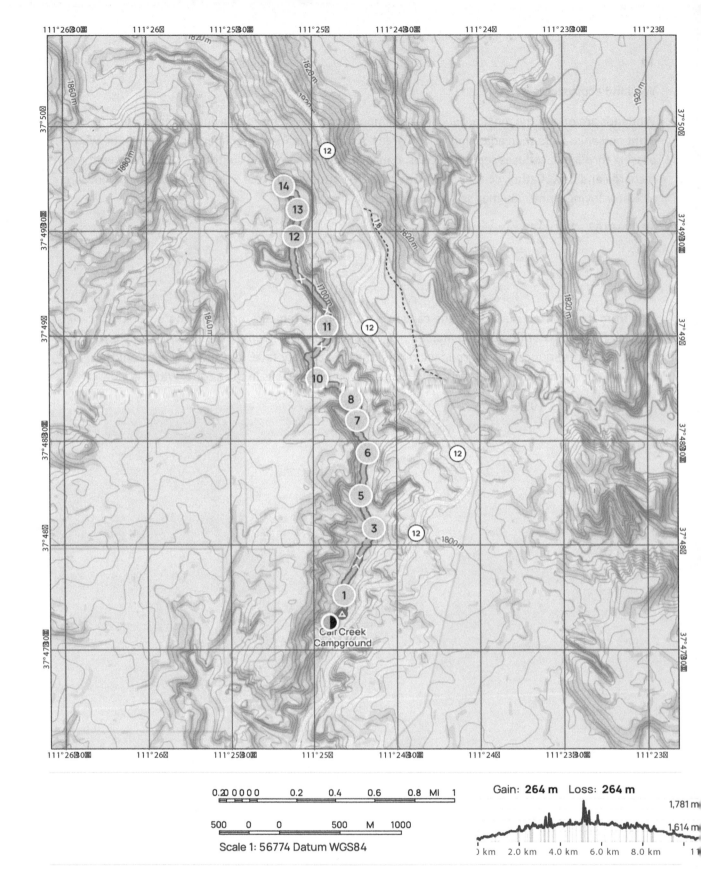

Gain: **264 m** Loss: **264 m**

0.20 0 0 0 0   0.2   0.4   0.6   0.8 MI 1

500   0   0   500 M 1000

Scale 1: 56774 Datum WGS84

1,781 m

1,614 m

0 km   2.0 km   4.0 km   6.0 km   8.0 km   1

Lower Calf Creek Falls
Escalante, UT

Start / End
37.79381, -111.41511

Upper Calf Creek Falls Trail

A spring provides the water source for the year-round flow of Calf Creek, which meanders along a shallow valley with several deep, clear pools before the upper falls, where the creek drops 88 feet over a cliff face at the head of Calf Creek Canyon. This deepens gradually for 2.5 miles south then doubles in size below the 126-foot lower falls. The upper cascade is not quite as spectacular and receives fewer visitors although it is quicker to reach and still well worth a look.

The Upper Falls trailhead is at the end of a short bumpy track off the west side of UT 12, near milepost 81, and is not signposted. It is reasonably popular though, presumably known by word of mouth or from guidebooks. The path to the falls is at first down a steepish slope of white slickrock marked by cairns of dark, volcanic pebbles then across flatter sandy ground to the canyon edge, with a total elevation loss of almost 600 feet. There is an easy route down a slope to the base of the falls though the main trail stays at rim level and ends at a group of clear pools just above the cliff edge. The distance is just over 1 mile, and a round trip can take less than one hour.

At the base of the falls is a large pool often deep enough for swimming, plus a second pool nearby beneath the junction of a (usually dry) tributary canyon that joins from the north. Most of the canyon floor from here downstream is quite overgrown with reeds, long green grass and bushes though hiking down the creek right to the top of the upper falls is possible - a combination of wading, boulder hopping and walking through the undergrowth. The best views of the upper waterfall are from beneath, or from the west side - it is easy to hop over the creek then climb up a slope and round the edge a little way.

Getting there

The unsigned spur road leading to the parking area is located on the west side of U12 between mileposts 81 and 82, 22.4 miles NE of Escalante. The short (200-300 yards) spur road is rough and sandy. If you are driving a low clearance vehicle park on the side of road at a pull out.

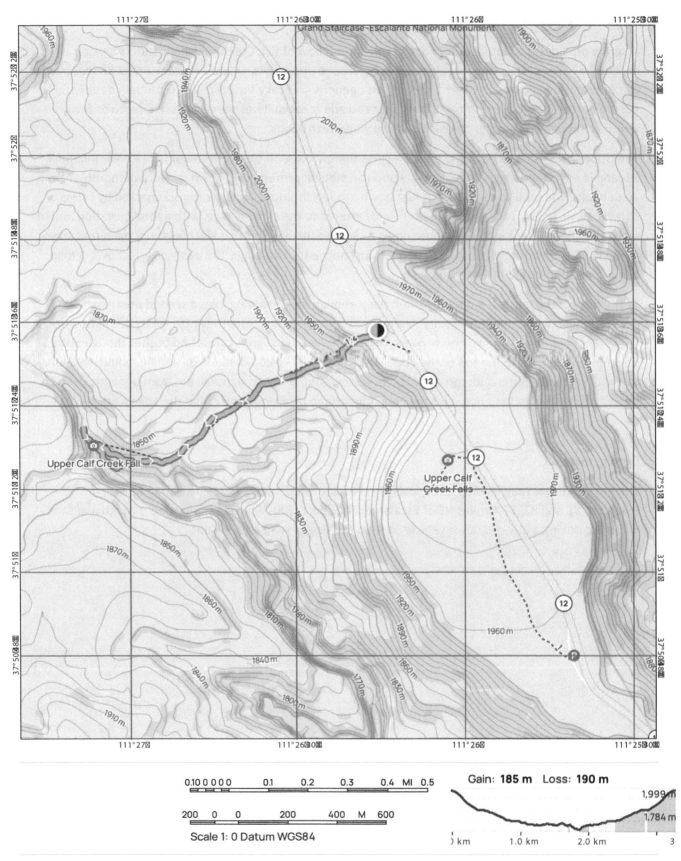

Upper Calf Creek Fall

Upper Calf Creek Falls

Gain: **185 m**   Loss: **190 m**

1,999 m

1,784 m

0 km   1.0 km   2.0 km   3

0.10 0 0 0 0   0.1   0.2   0.3   0.4 MI 0.5

200   0   0   200   400   M   600

Scale 1: 0 Datum WGS84

Upper Calf Creek Falls Trail
Boulder, UT

Start / End
37.85966, -111.43767

Escalante River Trail

Unlike many of its numerous tributaries, the 85-mile-long canyon of the Escalante River stays relatively wide all the way from Escalante town to Lake Powell, and a hike from start to finish can be completed in around 6 days, via a combination of wading in the river and walking along trails across the extensive grassy banks at either side. But most people come here for shorter trips, in particular the section between the town and the UT 12 crossing, since these are the only two points accessible by road.

This part of the canyon is 15 miles long so could be done in a day, if a car shuttle is available, however one option for an even shorter, there-and-back hike is the 2.5 miles of trail west of UT 12, as the scenery is the most varied; besides the river itself, flowing serenely through a corridor of trees, and the plentiful wildflowers on the surrounding meadows, this walk passes five features of note. These are Escalante Natural Bridge, a skyline arch, some Anasazi ruins, a petroglyph panel and a narrow tributary canyon (Sand Creek), which can be followed as far as desired, past pools, cascades and overhanging cliffs. All this stretch of the Escalante canyon, while not continuously sheer-walled, is bordered by the tall, extravagantly streaked cliffs of reddish Navajo sandstone that characterize all drainages in this region.

The Escalante River trailhead is one of the most popular in the area owing to its easy access and the variety of possible (overnight) trips that either start or end here, including to Pine Creek, Death Hollow, Sand Creek, The Gulch and Boulder Creek, yet even so, a typical day may see only 2 or 3 vehicles parked. The trailhead is located on the west side of the highway just north of the bridge over the river, in a tree-lined enclosure adjacent to a private residence.

At the trailhead, the canyon is relatively narrow but soon widens, becoming half a mile across, and remains similar for the 2.5 miles to Sand Creek, before narrowing again further west. The trail fords the river every half mile or so, the first crossing being just after the start, beyond a fork in the trail marked with a sign stating Lake Powell 70 miles, Escalante 15 miles. The cloudy Escalante River water is generally just a few inches deep and flows swiftly, across a floor of sand or small pebbles, and is always completely shaded by the bushes and trees that grow thickly along the edges and join together overhead, creating a cool, greenish passageway through the desert surroundings. The trail winds through woodland for a short distance but is soon traversing grassy, sandy flats - hot in summer - and sprinkled with cacti and many different species of wildflowers. The enclosing cliffs rise up to 400 feet above the river and are quite spectacular, especially on the south side where the sheer rock faces are streaked with wide, multi-colored bands of desert varnish. The north side of the canyon is less steep, the cliffs here split by benches and small ravines.

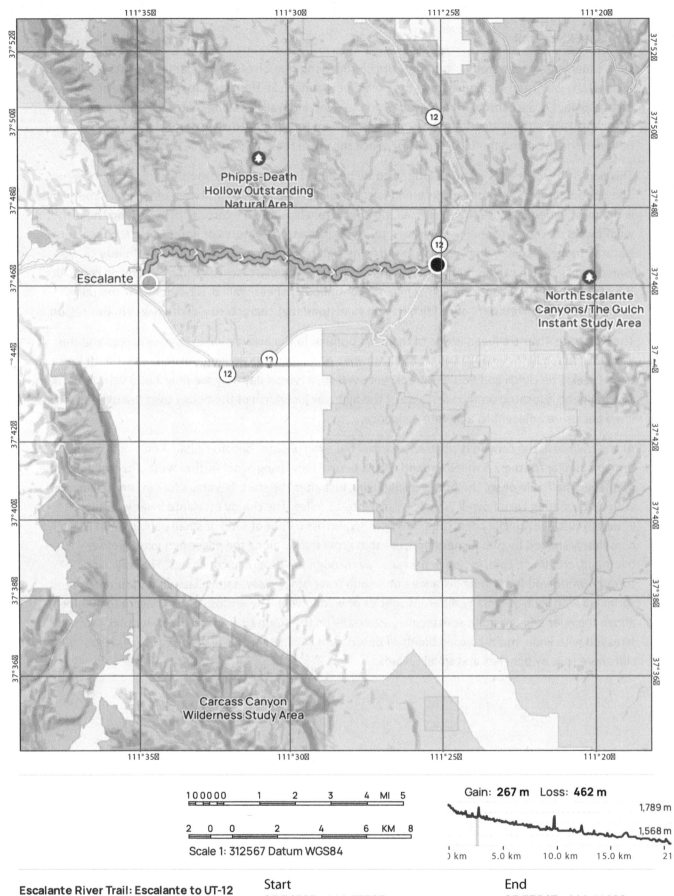

111°35☒   111°30☒   111°25☒   111°20☒

Phipps-Death
Hollow Outstanding
Natural Area

Escalante

North Escalante
Canyons/The Gulch
Instant Study Area

Carcass Canyon
Wilderness Study Area

100000   1   2   3   4   MI   5

2   0   0   2   4   6   KM   8

Scale 1: 312567 Datum WGS84

Gain: **267 m**   Loss: **462 m**

1,789 m

1,568 m

0 km   5.0 km   10.0 km   15.0 km   21

Escalante River Trail: Escalante to UT-12
Escalante, UT

Start
37.76787, -111.57797

End
37.77567, -111.41922

Escalante Natural Bridge

After rounding a few wide bends and crossing the river several more times, the path reaches the first attraction, 130-foot-high Escalante Natural Bridge. This is an arch rather than a bridge (created by erosion not water), though does resemble a real bridge, with a flat top and vertical, tapering supports. The arch has formed in the richly-colored red-orange rocks on the south side of the canyon and is parallel to a sheer cliff face, so the feature is most dramatic if viewed from behind, looking back north through the opening towards the opposite canyon walls - a location reached by walking up the short stream that runs from the arch, and climbing the boulder-strewn slope at the end.

This is a fun trail that requires multiple river crossings so be prepared to get your feet wet. It can be HOT and sandy in summer. along the south side of the canyon walking, you'll first come to the natural bridge, then to petroglyphs, then to a jughandle type arch all on the south side of the river, all fairly close together. for an easy added treat when done, walk to the southeast corner of the concrete bridge adjacent to the trailhead parking lot - there's an easily visible (but inaccessible) granary on the south side of the creek (directly below the formation Kiva Koffehouse sits on), viewable while standing on the pavement.

Waypoint

1

Ruins

Visible from dry land trail

37.77512, -111.45023

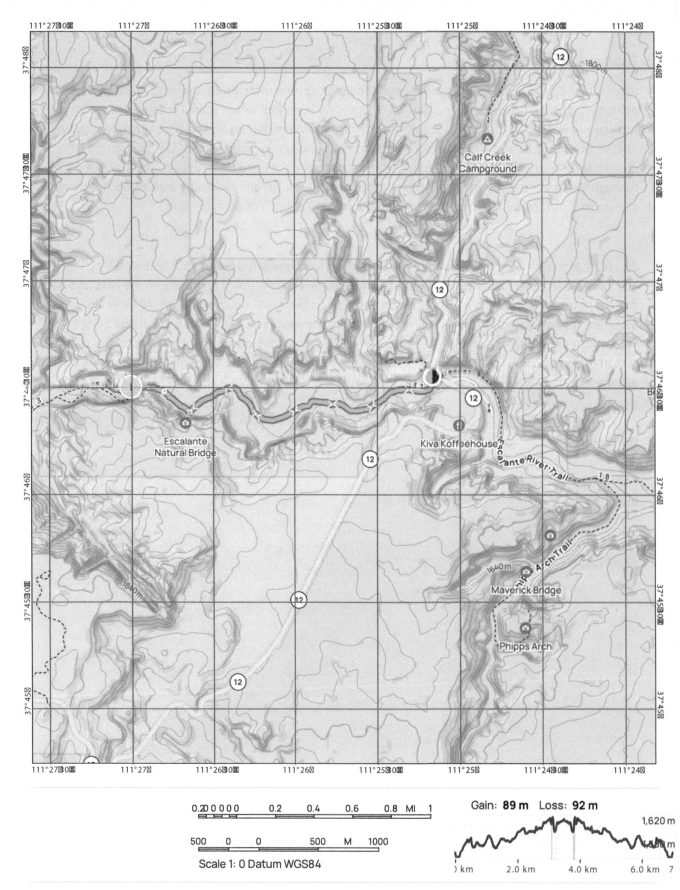

111°27′30″	111°27′	111°26′30″	111°26′	111°25′30″	111°25′	111°24′30″	111°24′	

37°48′

37°47′30″

37°47′

Calf Creek
Campground

37°47′30″

37°47′

(12)

37°46′30″

Escalante
Natural Bridge

Kiva Koffeehouse

Escalante River Trail

(12)

37°46′

(12)

1.8

37°46′

1840m

1640m

Phipps Arch Trail

Maverick Bridge

37°45′30″

(12)

Phipps Arch

37°45′

(12)

37°45′

| 111°27′30″ | 111°27′ | 111°26′30″ | 111°26′ | 111°25′30″ | 111°25′ | 111°24′30″ | 111°24′ |

0.20 0 0000   0.2   0.4   0.6   0.8   MI   1

500   0   0   500   M   1000

Scale 1: 0 Datum WGS84

Gain: **89 m**   Loss: **92 m**

1,620 m

0 km   2.0 km   4.0 km   6.0 km   7

Escalante Natural Bridge
Escalante, UT

Start / End
37.77587, -111.41952

Death Hollow Loop

At over 20 miles, Death Hollow is one of the longest Escalante River tributaries; a permanent stream flowing through a deep, richly colored Navajo sandstone canyon containing innumerable pools, cascades and small waterfalls, and for most of its length is quite enclosed, by vertical cliffs up to 500 feet tall. The drainage starts high on the forested slopes of Boulder Mountain at 9,000 feet elevation, descends steeply in the upper stretches then more gently lower down, joining the Escalante River at 5,400 feet, at a point half way between the town of Escalante and the UT 12 highway crossing.

A trip into Death Hollow can begin from either of the two locations along the Escalante River, or from two places further north - one is reached via the unpaved Hell's Backbone Road, usually passable between May and October, which crosses the very upper end of the canyon, after a drive of 23.5 miles from Escalante or 15.5 miles from UT 12. The other is via the Boulder Mail Trail - prior to the highway construction this was the main route between Escalante and Boulder, traversing much open slickrock while descending in and out of three major drainages including Death Hollow, which is reached after a walk of 8.2 miles from Escalante or 5.6 miles from a trailhead west of UT 12.

All these routes involve a long hike of one or more days, and/or a car shuttle, but a shorter option is a there-and-back hike into the lowest, deepest part of Death Hollow, accessed by descending into the Escalante River canyon just downstream of the confluence, after driving 1.6 miles along a dirt track that forks northwards off UT 12; this is the hike described below. Note there is another canyon in the Escalante area with a similar name, but quite a different character; Little Death Hollow is a much narrower drainage, a tight slot for a mile or so, and usually dry.

The unsignposted track leading towards the Escalante River leaves UT 12 between mileposts 66 and 67 in the middle of Big Flat, a sandy plateau covered by grass and scattered trees. The 1.6-mile road is level but narrow, and the surface is soft, so the track is subject to washouts after heavy rain, and is liable to be deeply rutted at any time. Keeping right at two junctions, the track ends at a rocky area on the rim of a short side ravine, with the Escalante River canyon visible beyond, enclosed by huge white domes and cliffs. This is a scenic and peaceful place to spend the night.

Most parts of the 700-foot-deep Escalante River canyon are too sheer to climb down, but the route used to reach the lower end of Death Hollow is relatively easy - a steep walk down a slickrock slope, requiring use of hands in just a few places. The directions are to head northwards along the west rim of the side drainage, descending in and out of a ravine then along flat benches and out to a white rock promontory overlooking the Escalante River and the lower end of the side drainage (which forms a short, very narrow slot canyon). Next is a traverse westward for a few hundred feet until the slope below becomes less steep, centered on a long vertical fault in the sandstone, which provides good footholds when descending. This leads most of the way down the cliffs, to a sandy gully, then the route is completed by climbing over a low ridge and walking down a sandy, boulder-strewn hill to the river, here flowing through a shady corridor of trees and bushes. Death Hollow joins the Escalante just half a mile upstream, and walking is easiest in the water, usually just a few inches deep, flowing over bare rock or pebbles.

The clear water in Death Hollow is a little deeper than in the Escalante upstream of the confluence, and faster-moving, but still (for most of the year) presents no problems when hiking up the canyon. Although the lower reaches are quite overgrown, with willow, cottonwood, oak, bamboo and poison ivy, plus a multitude of summer wildflowers, there are paths across the sand banks at either side of the streamway, so progress is relatively fast. Some parts of the creekbed are soft and sandy, separated by long stretches where the water flows over the bedrock, occasionally forming small cascades and waterfalls, sometimes with sheer, overhanging cliffs at one side. A small drainage joins from the west after 0.7 miles, flowing over a streaked cliff into a large pool, but otherwise there are no major landmarks in the lower canyon, which starts to curve around some sharp bends, whilst gaining height only slightly, hence lacking any deeper pools or bigger falls. These lower stretches are not particularly narrow though the canyon does constrict somewhat after about 2 miles, and for a short distance the creek is enclosed within a subway-like channel with potholes and cascades.

Waypoints

1

Camp 1

Camp on the creek!

37.82596, -111.53818

2

Camp 2

Even though this is a river confluence, the Escalante River is supposed to be dry, so this will probably be the last water we see on the trip.

37.78092, -111.50488

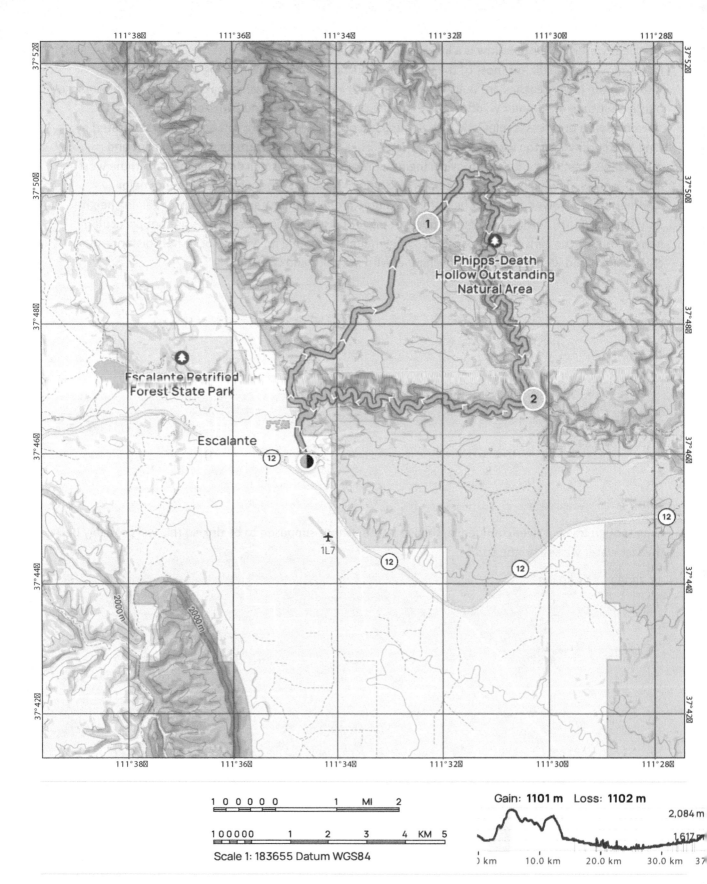

111°38⊠ 111°36⊠ 111°34⊠ 111°32⊠ 111°30⊠ 111°28⊠

37°52⊠
37°50⊠
37°48⊠
37°46⊠
37°44⊠
37°42⊠

Phipps-Death
Hollow Outstanding
Natural Area

Escalante Petrified
Forest State Park

Escalante

1L7

1 0 0 0 0 0   1   MI   2

1 0 0 0 0   1   2   3   4   KM   5

Scale 1: 183655 Datum WGS84

Gain: **1101 m**   Loss: **1102 m**

2,084 m

1,617 m

0 km   10.0 km   20.0 km   30.0 km   37

BMT - Death Hollow Loop
Escalante, UT

Start / End
37.76457, -111.57663

Bull Valley Gorge Trail

In the hilly, wooded country around the upper Paria River valley, Bull Valley Gorge is a relatively well-known canyon, yet quite far from a paved road. It can be quite testing to explore as there are several dryfalls to negotiate - the highest is 12 feet - plus depending on recent weather, pools up to 4 feet deep and long patches of sticky, clayish mud may be encountered. The reward for the effort needed is over a mile of a deep, narrow Navajo sandstone canyon, quite similar to Buckskin Gulch but with more variety of rock formations and colors. A unique extra feature was the wreck of a 1950s pick-up truck, wedged high above a section of narrows, which formed the base of the one road bridge across the canyon, though the truck was washed away in 2019, along with half of the bridge.

The easiest approach to Bull Valley Gorge is from the north end of the Cottonwood Canyon Road, the paved route to Kodachrome Basin State Park - to get there, turn off along a track signposted to Johnson Canyon (Skutumpah Road), across a stony creekbed, then drive about 9 miles on the mostly good quality road that does still have some steep sections, especially the ascent up a plateau near the start. The road fords several streamways, including Willis Creek (which has a year-round flow) and Sheep Creek beneath a dam, both of which may be impassable after heavy rain. The gorge is not signposted but the bridge over the canyon is quite an obvious feature. The canyon can also be reached from the south, starting along Johnson Canyon Road that joins US 89, and driving for 40 miles across Skutumpah Terrace

Bull Valley Gorge is very impressive when viewed from above, either side of the road bridge; it is about 100 feet deep, dark and narrow - in some places the edges are almost close enough to jump over. Mud, pools and boulders are clearly visible below, and the car wreck beneath the bridge can be seen by walking upstream a way and looking back. The surrounding land is hilly, but gently so; above the gorge is a low valley with a nearly flat floor, into which the sheer ravine cuts abruptly.

To explore the canyon, start by walking through a gate by the bridge and follow a faint path along the north side for about 15 minutes, until the gorge becomes shallow enough to jump down into. Turning back downstream, the channel deepens quickly, firstly by a 10-foot dryfall below a chokestone; a log may be in place to aid the descent. The gorge is narrow from the beginning and remains so until shortly past the road bridge. Rocks in the upper section are grey-white in color, solid, old and weathered with many narrow layers of different angles - similar to the nearby canyon of Round Valley Draw but slightly less pretty. If visiting after recent rainfall, this early part is likely to contain many pools and patches of sticky mud. The deepest wading required is generally around 3 feet - through either water or mud.

There are several other dryfalls to climb over, usually with water and mud beneath. One of 6 feet may also require a tree stump for assistance, and the tallest drop, of 12 feet, is not easily passed without using a rope; one may be left in place. This section of the canyon is liable to change after flash floods, however, so falls and chokestones may become more or less of a problem. The bridge is reached soon after the 12-foot dryfall, and seems a long way above, with the truck precariously wedged beneath a mass of rocks and tree trunks. Beyond this point, the canyon widens somewhat but still has sheer walls, and remains similar in appearance for another mile. Smaller pools and boulders provide minor obstacles until the cliffs become less vertical and the canyon is lighter and more open. Large pine trees begin to grow on sand banks above the streamway as Bull Valley Gorge meanders away south, joining Sheep Creek and eventually the Paria River. A round trip to this point takes from 2.5 hours, a hike which judging on the amount of footprints seems to be followed by one or two people each day in summer.

The pick-up truck was driven over the edge of the then narrow, wooden road bridge in 1954, an accident in which three men died. Their bodies were recovered but the truck was left in place, and the bridge that exists today was made by pushing large rocks and tree trunks over the wreck, forming a sturdy barrier about 15 feet thick.

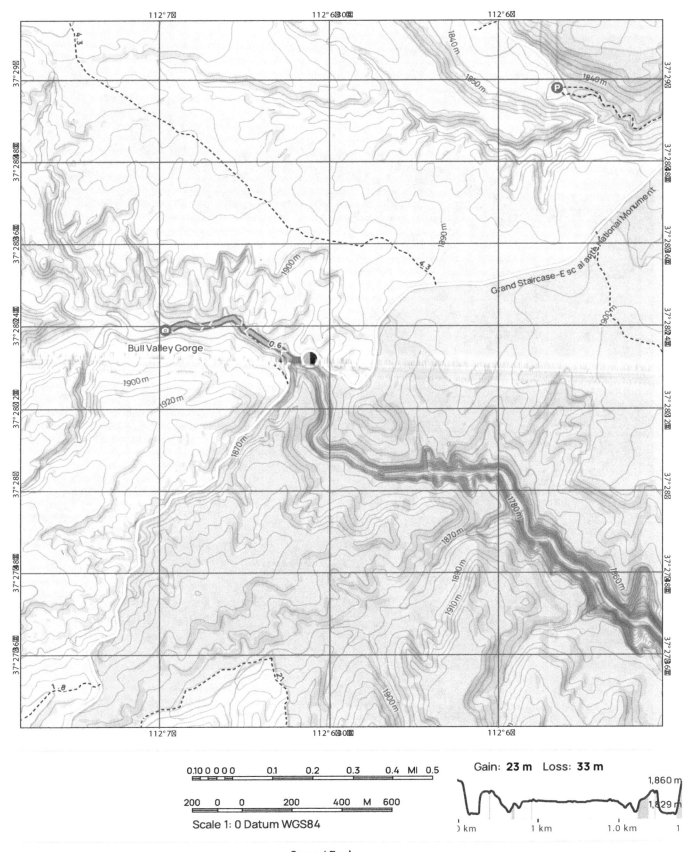

112°7 112°6 30 112°6

37°29
37°28 48
37°28 36
37°28 24
37°28 12
37°28
37°27 48
37°27 36

4.3

1840 m
1850 m
1840 m

P

1890 m

Grand Staircase–Esc al ante National Monument

4.3

1900 m

1900 m

Bull Valley Gorge

0.6

1900 m
1920 m
1870 m
1780 m
1870 m
1880 m
1910 m
1760 m
1900 m

0.10 0 0 0 0 0   0.1   0.2   0.3   0.4   MI 0.5

200   0   0   200   400   M   600

Scale 1: 0 Datum WGS84

Gain: **23 m** Loss: **33 m**

1,860 m

1,829 m

0 km   1 km   1.0 km   1

Bull Valley Gorge Trail
Alton, UT

Start / End
37.47201, -112.10933

Cosmic Ashtray

The Cosmic Ashtray, the Cosmic Navel, The Volcano and the Inselberg Pit, are some of the names given to an unusual geological feature in the vast Navajo sandstone plateau east of the Escalante River - a huge, circular, cliff-lined depression, filled with bright orange sand and centered on a rock pinnacle, resembling a dinosaur skull. The pit is 200 feet across and up to 60 feet deep, the result of erosion over the millennia by the prevailing southwesterly winds and the sands they carry. Inselberg is a German word meaning 'island mountain', here seemingly referring to the central pinnacle.

The official term of the formation is a cyclonic weathering pit, and this is considered to be the best example on Earth. It has formed in a gap between two minor peaks, along the ridge to the northeast of a large, low relief basin bisected by the various forks of Red Breaks; the wind blows across the basin and through the gap, where unevenness in the surface generates a circular motion, and this has led to the formation of the crater, which is still being actively enlarged. Having attained this great size, the hollow now draws in the wind due to differences in pressure, and thus the rate of enlargement increases.

The pit has a remote location, over eight miles from a paved road but may be accessed relatively easily, by driving 5.8 miles along a track, the unpaved Old Sheffield Road, and then a hike of 4 miles, across open sand and slickrock with only minor changes in elevation. Moqui steps have been constructed down in the lowest portion of the enclosing cliffs, allow scrambling down to the deep, coarse sand on the floor of the pit, while walking all around the rim allows viewing of the crater from all angles.

Old Sheffield Road leaves Highway 12 just south of its dramatic descent towards the Escalante River, and heads east, following the rim of a low plateau then crossing a large grassy area (Big Spencer Flats), up to a junction, with a track to the south. A sign advises that vehicles are prohibited from continuing, so the hike begins from here - initially along the eastward's continuation of the track until it approaches a sandy wash, 1.6 miles from the junction, then ends not far ahead in the vicinity of Spencer Canyon. The unmarked route to the pit is firstly across the wash and then southeastwards over slickrock at the base of a low ridge to the south, staying almost level at around 5,700 feet, past the upper ends of a few drainages, until, 3.8 miles from the road junction, veering due south below a white dome to the west, and ending 0.8 miles further with a climb of about 150 feet up a cross-bedded slope, approaching the pit from the east side, shortly after the bedrock changes color from orange to pale grey. The walls of the pit are high to the north and south, low again to the west, and here, the direction of the prevailing wind is evident from a sizable groove in the bedrock, enlarged and worn smooth by the Aeolian currents. The pit can also be reached by a much shorter walk, 0.8 miles, from the south, but this involves a ten-mile drive on a sandy road, the last few miles of which, from shortly before Harris Wash, require 4WD.

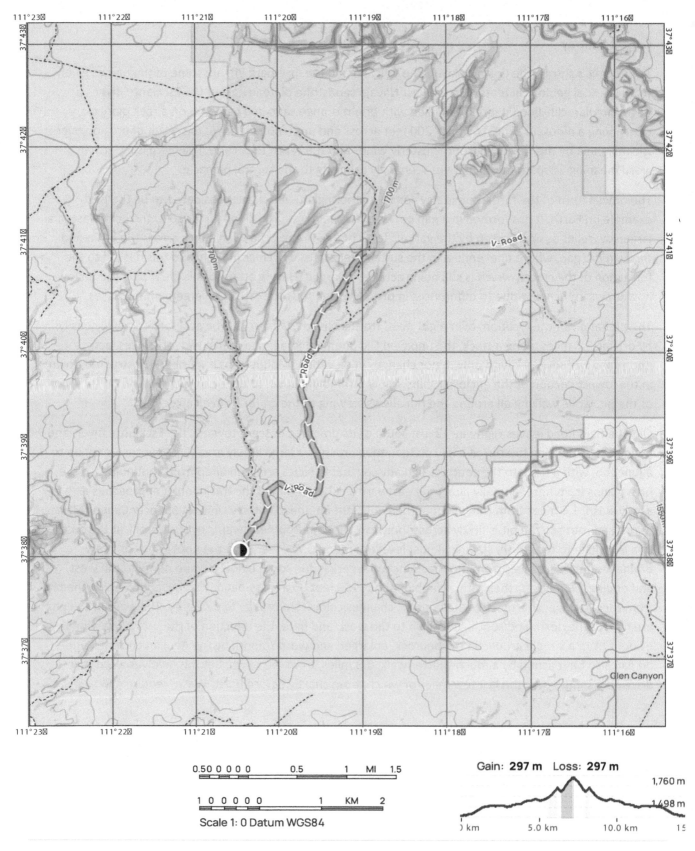

1700m

V-Road

Road

V-Road

1700m

1550

Glen Canyon

0.50 0 0 0 0   0.5   1   MI   1.5

1 0 0 0 0 0   1   KM   2

Scale 1: 0 Datum WGS84

Gain: **297 m**   Loss: **297 m**

1,760 m

1,498 m

0 km   5.0 km   10.0 km   15

The Volcano / Cosmic Ashtray
Escalante, UT

Start / End
37.63417, -111.34124

Willis Creek Narrows Trail

This is 0.9 miles to the end of the narrows, 2.1 miles to Sheep Creek, 5.6 miles to Bull Valley Gorge trail. Willis Creek flows a long way, from the base of the Pink Cliffs in Bryce Canyon National Park through high country at the edge of Grand Staircase-Escalante National Monument before joining Sheep Creek which eventually meets the Paria River. Several springs ensure its waters flow year-round, and just after the crossing of the Skutumpah Road - the unpaved route between Johnson Canyon and Cannonville, the creek enters a moderately deep gorge and passes through several short but very beautiful sections of narrows.

Unlike some other canyons in this area, Willis Creek is very easy to explore, with no obstacles of any kind, just a flat, stony streambed enclosed by shapely, delicately colored walls of Navajo sandstone.

The creek flows over the Skutumpah Road 7 miles south of the Paria River and about 2 miles from Bull Valley Gorge, at which point the stream is enclosed by a wide, shallow valley and is (usually) the only running water that crosses the road; it disappears tantalizingly into a swirl of sandstone just a few yards beyond. There is a large, flat area for parking and/or camping just north of the creek.

The depth of the clear, fast-flowing water is typically just 1-2 inches, and the canyon floor has no mud or potholes, just clean sand and small pebbles so walking is quite easy. Near the road, the creek drops 3 feet into a narrow sandstone channel which deepens gradually, the enclosing cliffs becoming up to 30 feet high. Occasional small waterfalls form where the floor drops over small chokestones, and the canyon has several quite lengthy curving, narrow passageways, nicely illuminated when the sun shines, and always very photogenic. After one mile the creek is joined by Averett Canyon from the north and thereafter becomes wider and more V-shaped. Pine trees and bushes grow around the streambed and the drainage remains similar in character for the next mile, to the confluence with larger Sheep Creek.

Two loop hikes are possible - either the 14-mile circuit of Bull Valley Gorge/Sheep Creek/Willis Creek (best done in this clockwise direction as the gorge is easier descended than ascended), a journey that includes 2 miles of road walking, or the much shorter 4-mile trip through Averett Canyon and Willis Creek. Averett has no narrow sections but is still quite pretty, and has the extra feature of a historic memorial, to a Mormon settler (Elijah Everett) who was killed by Indians in 1866. A dryfall near the junction with Willis Creek presents quite an obstacle so again this loop is easier done in this direction.

Family friendly walk in a creek through a slot canyon, excellent for hot days.

The approach road is not suitable for sedans as there's a steep, sandy hill just past Cannonville. Creek may dry out in late summer.

As with any slot canyon, DO NOT ENTER IF RAIN IS PREDICTED - flash flooding may occur from storms miles away (in this case, in Bryce Canyon National Park). call GSENM Cannonville (435) 826-5640 or Escalante (435) 826-5499 Visitor Center for more information.

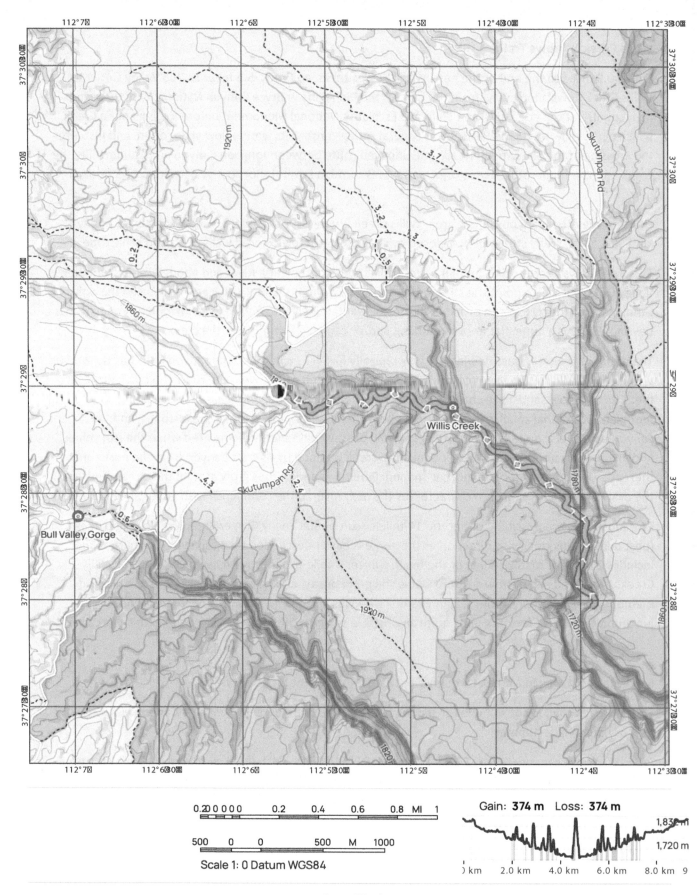

Willis Creek

Skutumpan Rd

Skutumpan Rd

Bull Valley Gorge

1920 m

1860 m

1780 m

1720 m

1920 m

1820

Gain: **374 m** Loss: **374 m**

1,832 m

1,720 m

) km   2.0 km   4.0 km   6.0 km   8.0 km 9

0.20 0 0 0 0 0   0.2   0.4   0.6   0.8   MI   1

500   0   0   500   M   1000

Scale 1: 0 Datum WGS84

Willis Creek Narrows Trail
Kanab, UT

Start / End
37.48293, -112.09651

Round Valley Draw

Many narrow canyons cut into the foothills of the Kaiparowits Plateau at the center of Grand Staircase-Escalante National Monument, and two of the Paria River drainage system have become quite well known - Bull Valley Gorge and Round Valley Draw. Waters of the latter flow south into the larger, wider Hackberry Canyon which then joins Cottonwood Creek, and this in turn meets the main river, a couple of miles south of the site of the old town of Paria.

The canyon formed by Round Valley Draw has about a half mile of deep, cool narrows through the light-colored, narrow layered Navajo sandstone rocks typical of this region. There are a couple of dryfalls to overcome but no major obstacles and the most interesting section can be explored in just 2 hours.

The canyon is reached by Cottonwood Canyon Road - the useful shortcut between US 89/Lake Powell and Bryce Canyon National Park. From the north end it is a 14-mile drive south then east, past the turning to Kodachrome Basin State Park, up and over several steep ridges to the streamway, which crosses the road a few miles before the frequently visited landmark of Grosvenor Arch. A side track is signposted to Round Valley Draw - this follows the shallow valley south for 1.5 miles, near to where the canyon deepens. There is one difficult stream crossing early on, then a second soon before the start of the narrows, just before which is a good place for parking, although the road does continue - it runs in the creek bed for a while then up the far side, on to the Rush Beds plateau and Booker Canyon. Off road vehicles can drive further down the creek, right to where the deep part of Round Valley Draw begins. In the late 1990s the BLM installed a trail register nearby, and it shows that on average one or two groups visit the canyon every day during the summer months.

After a 20-minute walk downstream from the parking area, the canyon proper starts abruptly - the creek cuts into the top of the Navajo sandstone layer via a three-stage drop of 15 feet, descent of which may be aided by a tree stump wedged between the rocks. This is easy enough going down but moderately difficult to climb back up. Most of the gorge thereafter is often muddy although usually without any major pools; a few days after rainfall the deepest water that requires wading is typically just 1.5 feet. The early narrows are particularly pretty with lots of thin tilted strata eroded into curves and ridges, and plenty of places where the sun illuminates the passageways and reflects along the canyon walls.

Soon after the entrance there is an alternative means of entry down the west side of the gorge - a near-vertical climb of about 30 feet using stepped rock ledges, which may be an easier egress point if there is no tree stump to aid the climb out of the upper end of the canyon. After here, Round Valley Draw deepens steadily, becomes quite dark in places with overhanging rocks partially hiding the sky above. A slightly wider section with many large fallen rocks ends in a drop of around 15 feet - an obstacle that may need a rope to overcome though at other times an easier route is possible underneath the final large boulder.

Next is the narrowest, deepest part of the draw, then the walls become less sheer and the canyon gradually opens out while continuing to deepen. Trees and bushes begin to grow at the sides and there is not much change for the next 1.5 miles, to the junction with Hackberry Canyon. Two climb-out routes along steep short, side canyons on the west side offer alternative ways back to the start point. A round trip (5.5 miles) to the Hackberry junction takes around 3 hours.

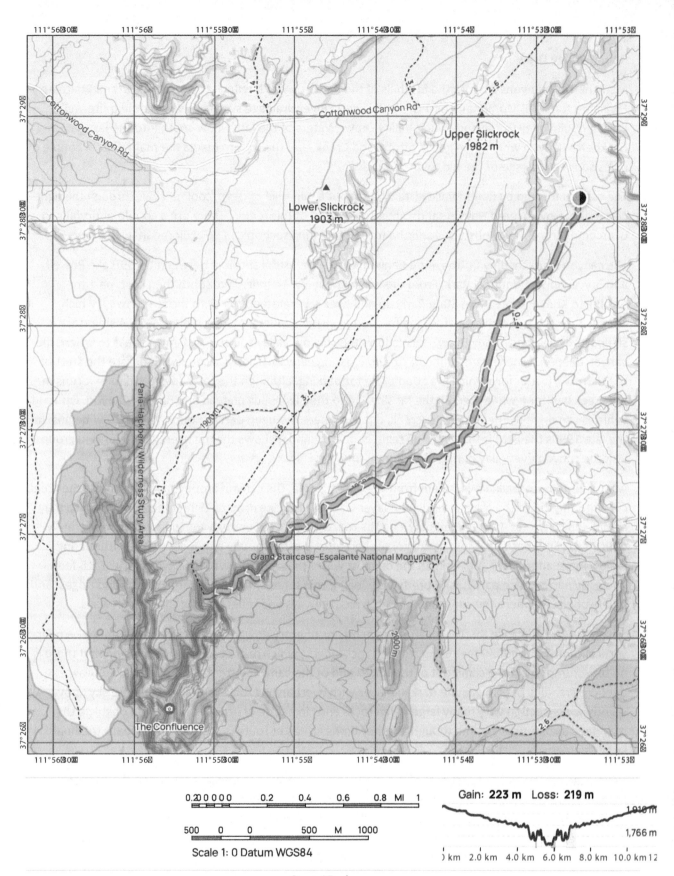

Gain: **223 m**   Loss: **219 m**

Scale 1: 0 Datum WGS84

Round Valley Draw
Kanab, UT

Start / End
37.47685, -111.88732

Yellow Rock

Along the unpaved Cottonwood Canyon Road in the west central region of Grand Staircase-Escalante National Monument, Yellow Rock is a low, smooth sided dome of swirling, multicolored Navajo sandstone, completely without any covering vegetation, and high enough to overlook many square miles of the surroundings. The far-reaching views are one attraction, but the main reason to visit is the amazing diversity of colors and textures; yellow is the main hue, but the sandstone is crossed by straight or wavy bands of many shades of red, pink and white, which combine with the thin-layered surface ridges to create a great variety of patterns. The rock has been known to locals for some time but has become a relatively popular destination since appearing in Michael Kelsey's Paria River book in 2004, and is typically visited by one or two dozen people each day in summer.

The summit of Yellow Rock lies close to the road and is reached by a short cairned route that climbs the west side of Cottonwood Canyon then crosses the slickrock slopes beyond. Besides the rock itself, the surroundings also have interesting features including jagged, heavily eroded pinnacles and elegant wave-like formations so although the rock can be seen in little more than one hour, a full day could be spent exploring. Other sites nearby include deep narrows along the lower end of Hackberry Canyon just to the north, and the Paria River valley a little further to the south.

Yellow Rock lies 31.7 miles from the north end of Cottonwood Canyon Road in Cannonville, but the shortest approach is from the south; a 14.3-mile drive from US 89, initially over grassy hills and then down into the Paria River valley, along the base of low cliffs for a few miles and over a saddle into the adjacent valley of Cottonwood Creek, which is bordered by the Coxcomb, a jagged ridge of upturned strata. Parking for the hike is on the east side of the road at the junction with a less traveled route (Brigham Plains Road) that climbs over the Coxcomb and crosses the high plateau beyond. Cottonwood Canyon Road can be rather rough at some times of year and is completely impassable after rainfall, but in dry conditions the route is usually fine for all vehicles. Other nearby trailheads, both with BLM notices (unlike Yellow Rock), are Hackberry Canyon 0.2 miles north and the Paria Box 2.5 miles south. There are many good places for free camping in the vicinity.

The valley of Cottonwood Creek is bordered to the west by a line of steep white cliffs, but a small side canyon immediately west of the parking area provides a route to the top of the escarpment; Yellow Rock rises up just beyond, mostly out-of-sight of the road but visible a little way south from the saddle between the Paria and Cottonwood drainages. The hiking route to the rock is west, through bushes and across Cottonwood Creek, which may be dry in the summer but for most of the year is a very shallow wash, flowing gently along a wide sandy corridor lined by cottonwood trees. Once at the mouth of the little ravine, a distinct path appears, ascending rather steeply up the north side of the ravine, around the head of a small valley and out to flat ground on the rim of the cliffs, where Yellow Rock appears directly ahead. The trail, partly cairned, crosses open, lightly vegetated terrain of sand dunes and slickrock to the south side of the dome, from where the summit is a short distance further. The path continues, less used, due west another 1.5 miles to a junction with the Paria Box Trail.

The summit of Yellow Rock is flat, and elongated, though the actual highpoint is towards the west. The northwest slopes seem to be more uneven and show less color variation; the best area is to the southwest, where the sandstone is smoother, colored contrasting shades of white, red and yellow, crossed by complex, swirling patterns of darker or lighter colors. These cut across the surface texture, which is thin-layered and angled, eroded into narrow, parallel ridges, best viewed early or late in the day when shadows enhance the appearance. Other parts of the rock surface are quite flat though may be cracked into neat polygonal shapes. The summit is the highest point for some distance and has spectacular views in all directions, over mountains, canyons, plateaus and ridges - west across the Paria River, north over Hackberry Canyon to other peaks including Castle Rock, and east over the Coxcomb. Most of the surroundings are similarly colorful, but less distinctive as the rocks are jagged and partly vegetated.

Yellow Rock is quite extensive, half a mile across, but it is not necessarily easy to find a good perspective for photography, as much of the surface looks the same, especially from a distance. The northeast side of the dome, while being generally less colorful - whitish rather than yellow - also has some good patterns, where the slickrock begins to slope down towards Hackberry Canyon. Other photogenic features include mottled patterns of distinct red spots in yellowish sandstone, sometimes ringed by light purple and gold. The low valley in front of the rock to the southeast, just north of the trail, has some delicate eroded formations like jagged fins and wavelike bowls.

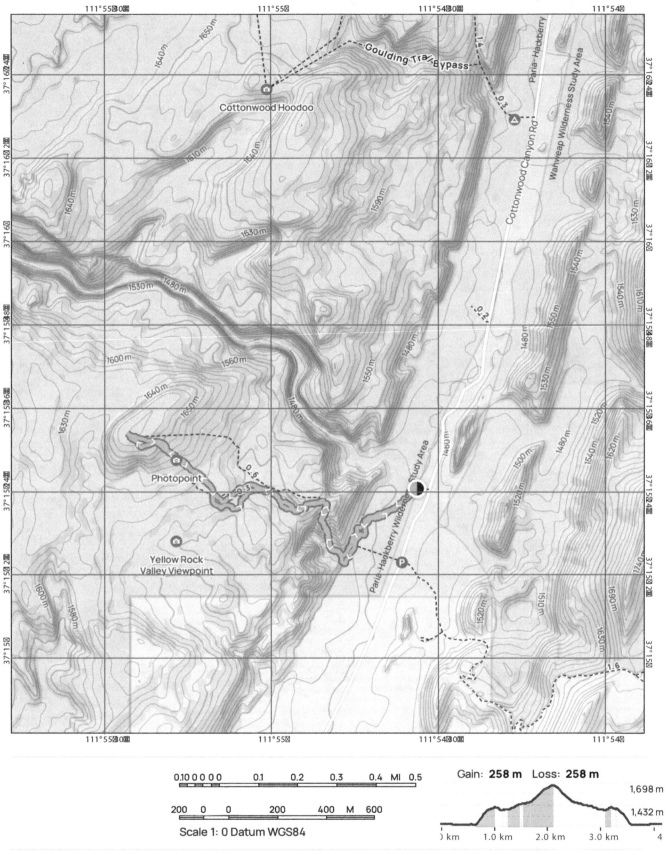

Yellow Rock
Alton, UT

Start / End
37.25676, -111.90941

Gain: **258 m** Loss: **258 m**

Scale 1: 0 Datum WGS84

Red Breaks Slot Canyon Trail

Harris Wash is a major Escalante tributary, and one that offers an easy route to the river - amongst the most popular hikes in the region, this 10-mile trip passes much fine red rock scenery without any obstructions, through a canyon that becomes deep but is never very narrow. Side canyons offer more of a challenge; the longest is Red Breaks which joins the wash close to its main trailhead and heads due north, cutting through various sandstone rock layers with colorful formations, a variety of erosional and water-carved features and with one extended narrows section that is quite testing to explore. This is a journey deep into the wilderness; the canyon is remote, quite pretty and offers total solitude.

The signposted side track to the Harris Wash trailhead joins the Hole-in-the-Rock Road from the east at mile 11. It passes a small reservoir on the right then traverses a flat, open area towards a small mesa where the route divides. The left fork is required here; this becomes quite bumpy, descending steeply along a ridge and into a small ravine, with two dry streambed crossings that may prove difficult for 2WD vehicles. The final section is along flat land beside the wash, past a corral beneath a sloping sandstone cliff with a series of Moqui steps cut into the rock. Most people camp/park here though the road does continue half a mile more, through a soft sandy area prone to flooding, and ends at the banks of the wash, which is wide, stony and usually dry since at this point the waters flow only after recent rainfall. Another track crosses the wash, heading north for several miles, and is sometimes used to reach the Cosmic Ashtray - a giant sandstone weathering pit - though the easier approach to this is from the north. The Harris Wash hike involves simply walking downstream towards the Escalante River, while Red Breaks is reached by crossing the wash and walking a short distance along the northwards track, which soon descends into the dry streambed at the lower end of the target canyon.

After a short distance the streambed becomes enclosed by reddish cliffs a few meters high but remains fairly wide and open, containing a lot of boulders, reeds, trees and bushes and occasional small dryfalls. The first major obstacle is encountered after 30 minutes walking - a vertical step of 20 feet, by-passed by climbing the walls on the east side. Several minor side canyons join the main ravine which cuts through various colorful layers of the Carmel formation, and has flat sections alternating with short eroded channels and pools as it erodes into the different strata.

The main narrows start after about one hour of hiking, where the wash enters the Navajo sandstone layer. The passageways are never very deep but are enclosed and quite interesting. The canyon here has frequent pools - usually just 1-2 feet deep - and several chokestones beyond which the canyon continues up to 10 feet higher up and so need careful climbing; in several places the chimneying technique is necessary. After the last such blockage, Red Breaks opens out and next are several shorter, less deep narrow channels separated by wider, sandy stretches. Travel through the narrows section can be avoided by scrambling up to a bench on the east side and walking along above the canyon.

Almost three miles from Harris Wash and after about 2 hours walking, the canyon divides - to the right, above a dryfall, is a narrowish passage that doesn't extend too far and is replaced by a shallow streambed that heads towards a butte on the horizon, across a wonderland of eroded rock domes and hoodoos. The main (left) fork soon ends in a pool and a 10-foot drop below a narrow passage; it is not possible to climb up here but beyond the canyon becomes deep and narrow once more, as can be seen by scrambling up the ridge between the two branches and traversing the slopes above.

Waypoints

1

Trailhead

37.63406, -111.34131

2

Bypass

37.66599, -111.34223

3

Dryfall

37.66736, -111.34247

4

Good Slots 1

37.67039, -111.34356

5

Good Slots 2

37.68006, -111.34868

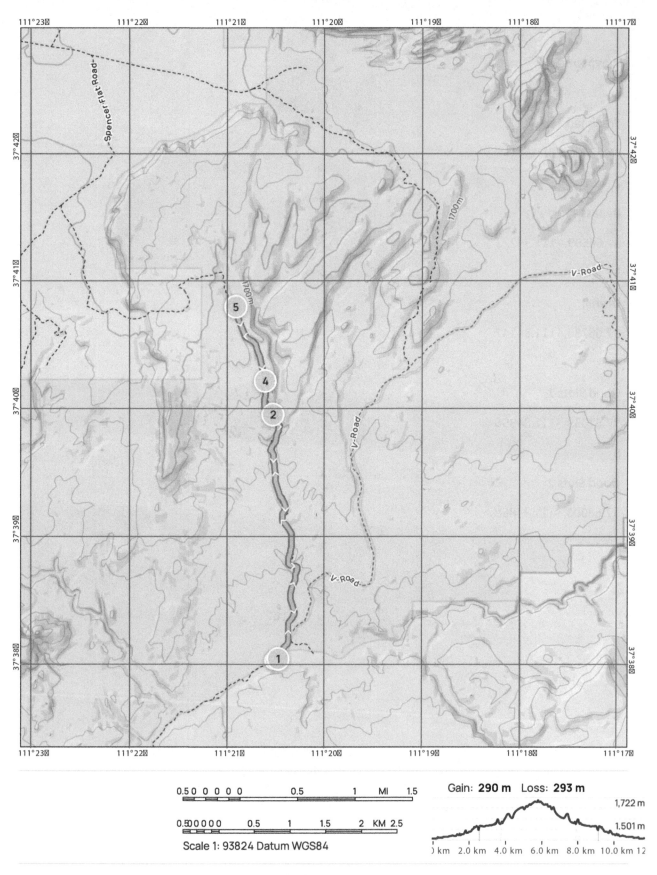

111°23⊠ 111°22⊠ 111°21⊠ 111°20⊠ 111°19⊠ 111°18⊠ 111°17⊠

37°42⊠
37°41⊠
37°40⊠
37°39⊠
37°38⊠

Spencer Flat Road
1700m
1700m
V-Road
V-Road
V-Road

5
4
2
1

0.50 0 0 0 0   0.5   1   MI   1.5

0.50 0 0 0 0   0.5   1   1.5   2   KM   2.5

Scale 1: 93824 Datum WGS84

Gain: **290 m**   Loss: **293 m**

1,722 m

1.501 m

0 km   2.0 km   4.0 km   6.0 km   8.0 km   10.0 km   12

Red Breaks Slot Canyon Trail
Escalante, UT

Start / End
37.63367, -111.34214

Cottonwood Narrows

The short narrows of Cottonwood Wash are easily explored and have become quite popular, since the entrance is right beside the access road, although this is not obvious and the canyon is easily missed. The approach is along the unpaved Cottonwood Canyon Road which follows close beside the wash for 25 miles, mostly in an open valley but the upper section of the creek flows through quite a narrow canyon, separated from the road by a thin strip of land formed by a steeply-angled layer of Navajo sandstone. This is one of the components of the Coxcomb, an elongated series of ridges running along one side of Cottonwood Canyon created by erosion of upwardly-pointing folded strata.

The entrance to the narrows is at the west side of Cottonwood Canyon Road, 22 miles from Cannonville and 25 miles from US 89, about 4 miles south of the turning to Grosvenor Arch. It is not signposted but is recognizable from a particularly colorful line of jagged red, orange and white rocks on the east side of the track (see 360-degree panorama), as it drops into a small valley formed by a minor drainage that flows from the east, under the road and through a narrow gap into the main canyon. There are plenty of parking places, on both sides of the road.

The narrows may be entered either along the bed of the side drainage or through an opening in the cliffs 100 feet south. The canyon is interesting for a few hundred yards upstream and for one mile downstream, although the upper part is best - a few places are as narrow as any other of the Paria tributary canyons, with some minor dryfalls and pools and plenty of nice rock formations. Beyond the end of this section, the wash continues northwards for many more miles through a shallow, boulder-strewn valley.

Turning south at the entrance, the wash becomes quite deep and generally rather wide - for long distances sandbanks with trees and bushes line the streamway on both sides but there are also a few dark narrow passages, enclosed by high, vertical cliffs of Navajo sandstone streaked with desert varnish. After 20 minutes walk the canyon bends 90 degrees to the east and cuts through the ridge separating it from the road, and thereafter flows south through a much wider valley. The hike is completed by walking up the road back to the parking area, and the round trip to both parts of the narrows takes just one hour.

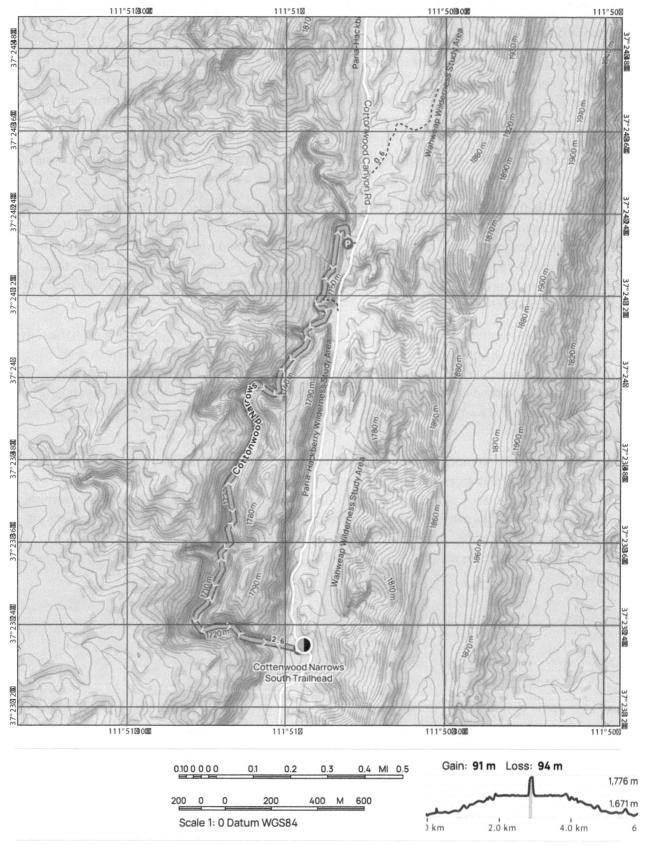

Paria-Hac Kb

Cottonwood Canyon Rd

Wahweap Wilderness Study Area

0.6

P

1750 m

Cottonwood Narrows

1790 m

Paria-Hackberry Wilderness Study Area

Wahweap Wilderness Study Area

1720 m

1780 m

1790 m

1720 m

1720 m

2.6

Cottenwood Narrows
South Trailhead

0.10 0 0 0 0   0.1   0.2   0.3   0.4 MI 0.5

200   0   0   200   400   M 600

Scale 1: 0 Datum WGS84

Gain: **91 m**   Loss: **94 m**

1,776 m

1,671 m

0 km   2.0 km   4.0 km   6

Cottonwood Narrows South to North Trailhead
Kanab, UT

Start / End
37.38915, -111.84907

Phipps Arch Trail

Most Escalante canyons are a long way from paved roads and need some effort to reach, but not Phipps Wash, as this is never more than two miles from UT 12, though still far enough away to escape completely from any traffic noise. It is not the most spectacular canyon in the area and has no especially narrow parts yet is very popular owing to the relatively easy access, and illustrates the different character of canyons in this region, changing from a sandy drainage winding through slickrock, to a sheer red-walled gorge, then to an overgrown, bushy ravine where a stream begins to flow. One added feature of interest is 100-foot-wide Phipps Arch, located high in the cliffs above a side valley.

The lower end of Phipps Wash meets the Escalante River 2 miles downstream from the UT 12 crossing and can be accessed from the highway via an easy trail. The upper end begins at the edge of Little Spencer Flat, a plateau crossed by the Old Sheffield Road - a route that leaves UT 12 between mileposts 70 and 71 and is also used to reach Big Horn Canyon and other nearby drainages, though it becomes increasingly sandy further east. There are various places to camp along here, including one area just off the main road, so handy for overnight stops when traveling cross country. The highway is very little used at night. The beginning of Phipps Wash is about 2 miles along the track, nearly opposite the start of Big Horn Canyon, but the hike can begin anywhere before this, just by walking east to the first side drainage then following this downstream.

The parking/camping area close to UT 12 is as good a place as any to start, and from here the route is southeast, towards a gap in the steepish cliffs that form a barrier to the slickrock beneath, this being 0.3 miles from UT 12. The slope relents here allowing for a descent to a sandy area then further down into a side drainage of the main canyon. The surrounding land is dotted with cacti, bushes and wildflowers, especially Indian Paintbrush, but is mostly bare of vegetation. This side canyon has a few short dryfalls and seasonal pools then a big drop off, passed on the right side, shortly before the junction with the main channel of Phipps Wash. Large cliffs streaked by desert varnish soon rise on the east side then, after a wide area, the left side also becomes enclosed and a stream being to flow, causing the canyon to be quite overgrown by cottonwood trees and bushes. Eventually the walls open out as Phipps meets the Escalante River flood plain, though the actual river is another third of a mile more, flowing swiftly though a corridor of reeds and trees.

Although large, Phipps Arch is well hidden at the top of the cliffs to the east of the wash, and is not visible from the main drainage. There is no obvious clue to its whereabouts, except perhaps for a trail of footprints, but it is situated along the only significant east-side tributary joining in the enclosed part of the main canyon, approximately half way to the Escalante River. The arch is reached by a 10-minute walk from the wash, climbing quite steeply up the sloping slickrock on the left of the side canyon heading for a small gap between the highest parts of the sandstone peaks - the span is about 0.3 miles from the Phipps Wash streamway, and perpendicular to it. Also quite well hidden, though easier to reach, is Maverick Natural Bridge, a little way up a side drainage on the other side of the main wash. This has a span of about 20 feet, often with a pool underneath, and is quite shaded by trees and bushes.

Waypoint

1

Phillips Arch   37.75638, -111.41017

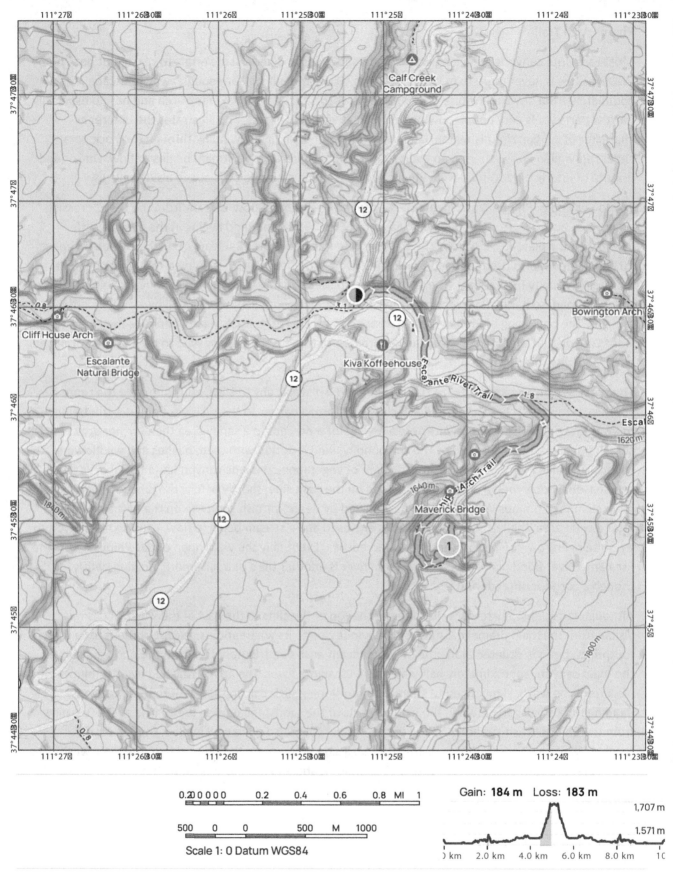

| 111°27 | 111°26 30 | 111°26 | 111°25 30 | 111°25 | 111°24 30 | 111°24 | 111°23 30 |

Calf Creek
Campground

Bowington Arch

Cliff House Arch

Escalante
Natural Bridge

Kiva Koffeehouse

Escalante River Trail

1.8

Escal

1620 m

1640 m

Phipps Arch Trail

Maverick Bridge

1840 m

1800 m

Scale bar:
0.2 0 0 0 0 0   0.2   0.4   0.6   0.8 MI   1

500   0   0   500   M   1000

Scale 1: 0 Datum WGS84

Gain: **184 m** Loss: **183 m**

1,707 m

1,571 m

0 km   2.0 km   4.0 km   6.0 km   8.0 km   10

Phipps Arch Trail
Boulder, UT

Start / End
37.776, -111.41951